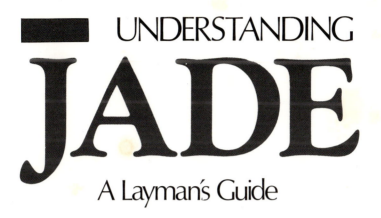

UNDERSTANDING JADE

A Layman's Guide

LEE SIOW MONG

Times Books International
Singapore • Kuala Lumpur

Cover Illustration

☐ *White Jade Citron Fruit (called Buddha's Fingers) with yellow patches*

© **1988 TIMES BOOKS INTERNATIONAL**
Times Centre
1 New Industrial Road
Singapore 1953

2nd Floor
Wisma Hong Leong Yamaha
50 Jalan Pencala
46050 Petaling Jaya
Malaysia

All rights reserved. No part of this publication may be reproduced, stored in any retrieval system, or transmitted, in any form or by any means, electronic, mechanical, photocopying, recording or otherwise, without the prior permission of the copyright holder.

Printed by Kim Hup Lee Printing Co. Pte Ltd

ISBN 9971 65 4962

CONTENTS

□ *Pale green jade crab*

Introduction 5

1   What is Jade? 9
    The Stone Par Excellence 9
    Colours and Varieties of Jade 10
    Sources of Jade 13
    Authoritative Writings 16

2   Jade in Mythology 21
    The Western Godmother and Kunlun Mountains 21
    Confucius and the Jade Book 23
    Jade in Alchemy and Medicine 24
    The Jade Hare 25
    The 'Most Precious Piece of Jade' 26
    Jade in Literature 29

3   Jade and its Qualities 33
    Identification of Jade 33
    What is Good Jade? 35
    Old and New Jade 36
    Colour Change 40
    Faking Jade 41
    All Jade Pieces Can Be Carried 42
    Enjoyment of Jade 43

□ *White jade coin with the reign of Cheng-te*

4 Historical Jade 45

    Jade 'Carving' 47
    The *Gui* 47
    The *Cong* 49
    Burial Jade 50
    The Cicada 51
    The Jade Pig 52
    The *Weng Zhong* 52
    Tallies *Fu* 54

5 Jade and Mortals 59

    Another Famous Jade Seal 61
    Pendants 63
    The *Gang Mao* 64
    Military Tallies 66

6 Jade as Ornament and Art 71

    The Jade Hairpin 71
    Jewellery 73
    Personal Jewellery 76
    Jade in Art and Art in Jade 78
    Snuff Bottles 93
    The Four Spiritually Endowed Creatures 94
    Jade's Place in Antiquities 94

☐ The jade seal of Zhao Fei Yan.

Epilogue   96

Bibliography   97

☐ The head of the Joo-I showing the Double Happiness carving in relief.

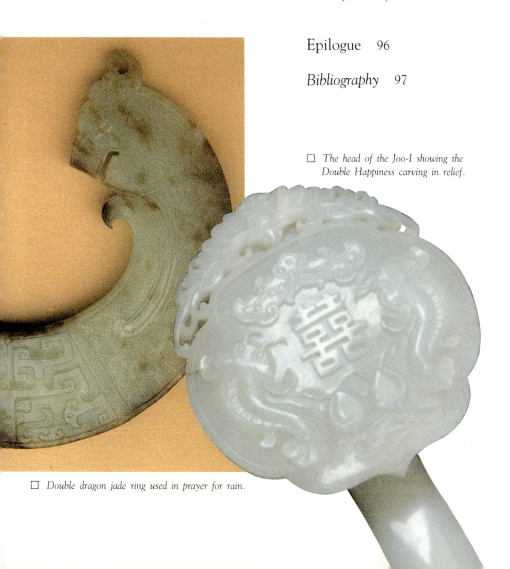

☐ Double dragon jade ring used in prayer for rain.

This book is dedicated to
my white jade goose
who has accompanied me
around the world seven times

□ *White jade goose. Note the three dimensional design of the animal carving.*

Introduction

C hinese antiquarians have written few books on jade, and historical records are fewer. Scientific studies were non-existent until the last hundred years or so (as the Chinese did not concentrate as much on the scientific aspects of their universe as on the moral ones).

Jade is a product of Nature produced by the interaction of the "Essence" of the great mountains and rivers and the "Breath" of Heaven and Earth. As such, it has been greatly valued and revered for thousands of years. However, no written records were left for posterity until many thousands of years later in the Song Dynasty, 10th/12th century A.D. when antiquarians attempted to study this most fascinating stone. By this time millions of jade objects had been left behind by the ancients. The antiquarians made their observations and conclusions on the basis of clever conjecture and occasional clear evidence. Thus the authority of these studies cannot be relied upon.

More scientific studies on the subject have been produced by such well known personalities like Heber R. Bishop, S.W. Bushell, B. Laufer, H. Fisher and many others. These writings have covered much new ground and provided more information and opinions on the early uses of jade.

My purpose in writing this book is not to repeat what has already been studied and written by these writers and the Chinese antiquarians, but to deal with the subject from a different angle such as that seen by the average Chinese who looks upon this "Stone Par Excellence" which Nature has given him to enjoy, treasure and cherish.

Understanding Jade

The numerous legends and stories concerning jade provide endless joyous reading and wonderment. The varied jade objects such as personal seals and other identifiable possessions of men and women in Chinese history are worth mentioning because they are real, but little is known about them.

The story of the jade heritage must be told or it will soon be lost forever. The philosophical and aesthetic appeal of jade is enjoyed or has the potential to be enjoyed by everyone, whether young or old, rich or poor.

The Chinese, for whom this stone is most important, have a special relationship with this colourful and meaningful stone. It is for this reason that I have decided to write this book with the many illustrations to provide an insight into the enjoyment of jade in the Chinese mind. There is hardly an object in this world which has not been carved in jade by the ingenious jade craftsmen, and the varied illustrations in this book attempt to prove this point. To write this book is to share the endless joy of over half a century's experience of jade with those who may read this book.

☐ *The varied design of white jade snuff boxes with different stoppers: made of coral (2nd from left), rose quartz (1st and 3rd from left) and silver carving of a frog (extreme right).*

Introduction

☐ *Jade bird. The dark patches of colour are due to long periods of burial in the earth.*

Understanding Jade

□ *Pale green jade pendant carved with the Gods of Harmony and floral designs.*

WHAT IS JADE ? 1

The Stone Par Excellence

For thousands of years jade has been the stone par excellence in Chinese civilization. It is the second most important material after bronze in the history of Chinese culture. No other stone has played as important a part in Chinese mythology, religion, philosophy, folklore, social life and art.

In very ancient times the term jade '*yu*' was represented by a pictograph of three strips strung together thus 王 . From the numerous jade pendants recovered through the centuries, it is quite clear that the term '*yu*' covered a large number of semi-precious crystalline stones belonging to the agate, fluor and quartz families. The Chinese characters for members of these families all have a jade radical on the left side of the character signifying that they belong to the jade family, but jade alone is simply represented by the character (*yu*), which mineralogists have identified as jadeite and nephrite.

A black variety of jadeite, obtained principally in Burma, has been identified as chloromelanite; some black jade carvings are still extant today. Without making this description of jade look like a writing on mineralogy, it would suffice to say that 'black' is a colour among the many colours of jade, for which the Chinese have specific terms, impossible to translate into their English equivalents. Basically, nephrite is a silicate of calcium and magnesium with the chemical formula $CaO.3MgO.4SiO_2$ and jadeite is a silicate of sodium and aluminium with the formula $Na_2O.Al_2O_3.4SiO_2$.

Understanding Jade

Colours and Varieties of Jade

I have said earlier that in ancient times the term jade included many varieties of semi-precious crystalline stones whose names have a jade radical on the left side of the character. Today the two varieties which are called '*yu*' are actually nephrite and jadeite. Nephrite is 'soft jade' 软玉 (*ruan yu*), and jadeite is 'hard jade' 硬玉 (*ying yu*). Nephrite has a hardness of about 6 and specific gravity of 2.9 to 3.1. Jadeite has hardness of about 7 and specific gravity of 3.3. Diamond has a hardness of 10. Both nephrite and jadeite are white when pure and fuse easily, nephrite reducing itself to a grey slag and jadeite to a grey ash.

The colours of jade depend on the minerals present in it; they represent all the colours of the rainbow or a spectrum of light. The 'Jade Record' 玉纪 (*yu ji*) written in the nineteenth century says there are nine colours in jade:

1. Blackish blue	瑿蓝	(resembling settled water)
2. Bright green	碧青	(resembling settled foam)
3. Moss green	瑾绿	(resembling fresh moss)
4. Yellow	璷黄	(resembling kingfisher feather)
5. Red	玵赤	(resembling chestnut)
6. Purplish red	琼紫	(resembling cinnabar)
7. Red	璊	(resembling congealed blood)
8. Black	瑎	(resembling ink)
9. White	瑳	(resembling cut fat)

The Chinese characters are impossible to translate, but they are included in the text here as a matter of interest to show how complicated the colours of jade are. Each of these nine colours has its own variations of shade giving rise to more intricate descriptions like 'baby's face' 孩儿面 , 'date skin red' 枣皮红 , 'parrot green' 鹦哥绿 , 'chicken blood red' 鸡血红 , 'egg-plant purple' 茄皮紫 , 'mutton fat' 羊脂 , and so on. It is also recorded in the Jade Record that there exists a type of 'fragrant jade' 香玉 , which is the result of jade having been buried in the earth for a long time in constant contact with some fragrant material. This type of buried jade continues to emit fragrance years after recovery from the earth.

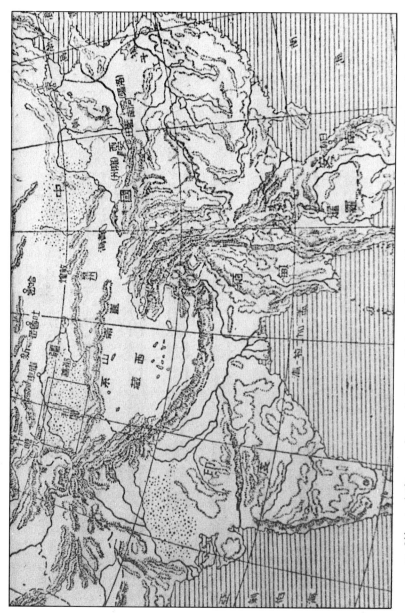

□ *Old map of China stretching to the Western Regions i.e. Sinkiang. The rectangle encloses the 120,000 sq. miles of jade producing country.*

Understanding Jade

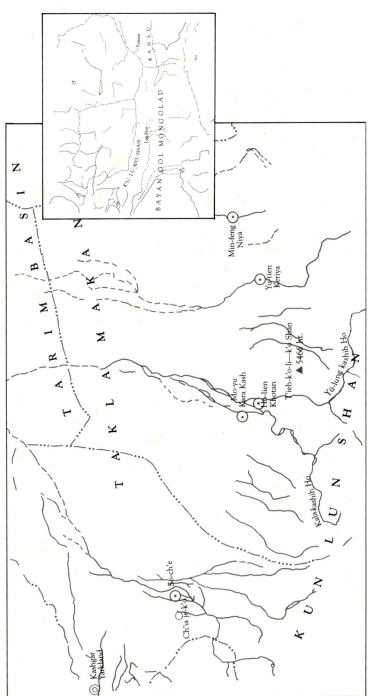

☐ The rectangle showing jade producing areas in the previous map. Within this area are big rivers like the Niya, Kurung Kash, Karakash, the Yarkland Daria which begin in the Kunlun mountains. They bring down jade boulders during the summer which are collected in the autumn when the torrential rains subside. The Gobi Desert is also included in this area.
Beyond this rectangle, smaller jade producing areas stretch eastwards and northwards taking in the Lobnor area right to the border of Kansu Province where the westernmost gateway from Kensu to Sinjiang after the Great Wall of China is called Yumen, meaning Jade Gateway.

Sources of Jade

Although in Chinese history it is said that the best and most beautiful jade comes from Lantian 蓝田 in Shanxi Province, and the *Shan Hai Jing* 山海经 (Hill and River Classics) records over two hundred places producing jade, there is little evidence of jade having been mined in China in any quantity. There are, however, many relics of jade objects dating back to over two thousand years, but the jade is of a different variety from that mined in Chinese Turkestan or elsewhere outside China. We can therefore only assume that there must have been jade mines in China which had been exhausted a long time ago. Research into jade mined in China and the ancient uses of jade have been made more difficult by the scarcity of work or writings on the subject. Studies made by antiquarians of the Song dynasty, twelfth century A.D., are at best only conjectures on this most illustrious of precious stones. Their work and writings were applaudable since they were born a few thousand years after the 'Golden Age' of jade in Chinese civilization and had to start with practically nothing.

The main supply of jade comes from Chinese Turkestan (Sinjiang) 新疆 , mainly white; and the coloured variety, *feicui* (翡翠) from Burma. For a long time craftsmen worked on jade from these two sources. Today there is jade from New Zealand, India, and some European countries.

Many legends of jade revolve around the Kun Lun mountains. This enormous mountain range between Sinkiang and Tibet has long been the site of jade explorations. Jade mining has been going on for centuries on the lower ranges on the side of Sinkiang. Rivers that originate in this mountain range carry boulders and pebbles of jade downstream during the rainy season. It is on record that around Khotan in Sinkiang are three rivers whose source is a river in the Kun Lun mountains running west for 1,300 li's (3 li's approximately to a mile). At Niu Tou Shan (牛头山) this great river divides into three smaller ones – one called the White Jade River, 30 li's east of Khotan; the second, Green Jade River, 20 li's west; and the third, Black Jade River, 7 li's west of the Green Jade River. Although these three rivers come from the same source, the colours of the jade found in them are different because of the difference in soil type of the river-bed. Each year during the summer months, the melting snow in the mountains bring torrents of water and with it jade boulders. When the torrential rains subside, the waters of the river recede making it safe for the collection of jade.

Understanding Jade

☐ This mountain lake called the Jade Pond is said to be part of the abode of the Western Godmother, Xi Wang Mu. This is part of the Tien Shan arm of the Kunlun range in the north which rises to varying heights between 3,000 and 5,000 metres. The lake is sometimes described as the Lake of Gems and is 100 li's long and 50 li's wide.

What is Jade?

☐ *The windswept upper regions of the Kun Lun mountains. This enormous mountain range branches to the north, east and southeast of China under various names. Practically all the primeval mountain ranges in China originate here.*

Jade is mined to a depth of some twenty feet or more, or simply found on riverbeds in various sizes (ranging from the size of little pebbles to large boulders of several hundred pounds in weight) and various colours. Normally the outer skin is a crusty brown and the crystalline part is inside. It takes a trained eye to recognise a jade boulder and to determine its colour and quality below the brown crusty skin. Some of the pebbles and boulders have been washed down mountain streams into the river beds.

For a long time the collection of jade from the rivers was also a government affair in addition to the industry of private enterprise. Teams of 20 or 30 collectors each were commandeered by one officer. These collectors were natives of Sinkiang. Each time a collector found a piece of jade in the river he stepped on it and announced his find. The soldiers on the river banks beat a gong and the officer marked the find in red in his records. The collection was thus rigidly controlled.

Understanding Jade

It was said that jade belonged to the *Yang* (male) element and that women were used as collectors as they embodied the *Ying* (female) element of the Chinese universe. These women were usually completely naked and it was believed that the jade in the river beds were attracted by the Ying element thus rendering them less elusive. Sometimes the work was done on moonlight nights. The jade could be seen more clearly because of the luminous glow they gave off.

Apart from the rivers, jade mining also took place on land. Jade is usually found about 10 feet or more below the surface. River beds can also be dug for jade and it is said that the jade thus found in the White Jade River (Yurung Kash) is the best variety. Places like Lob Nor and Kuku Nor in the same region are also jade mining areas.

Private mining expeditions for jade are still carried out today. It is reported to be a very profitable venture – production costs only take up 30% of the profit under normal conditions.

Authoritative Writings

For a long time the monumental works *Kao Gu Tu* (考古图) by Lu Da Ling (吕大临) in the late eleventh century, *Po Ku Tu* (博古图) compiled during the reign of Xuan He in early twelfth century, *Gu Ku Tu Pu* (古玉图谱) by Long Da Yen (龙大渊), also early twelfth century, of over one hundred volumes where the illustrations were said to have been drawn by such great artists as Liu Song Nian (刘松年), Ma Yuan (马远), Xia Kui (夏珪) and the *Gu Yu Tu* (古玉图) by Zhu Jek Ming (朱泽民), early fourteenth century, were considered the authorities on jade. These have since been discounted as being unauthentic and confused. Only the work by Wu Da Zheng (吴大澂) (1834-1902) known as *Gu Yu Tu Kao* (古玉图考) in four volumes, is acclaimed by Chinese scholars as authoritative and reliable. The drawings in these four volumes are of pieces in Wu's personal collection and are rendered by his brother Wu Da Zhen (吴大桢), an artist of great repute. These four volumes are by no means perfect. Further studies on jade made by Bishop, Kunz, Bushell and Laufer, who used Wu's writings as their basis, have further enriched our present knowledge on the subject.

What is Jade?

☐ *An old print of the White Jade River where teams of workers look for jade supervised by soldiers and officials on the bank. The moon in the print suggests that the activity takes place at night.*

☐ Another old print of the Green Jade River north of a branch of the Kun Lun range outside Khotan. It shows naked women 'fishing' for jade in the river.

What is Jade?

☐ In 1906 A. Stein made two expeditions to Sinkiang and discovered many wooden tablets at the Niya River near Khotan. These wooden tablets were inscribed with words showing that they were presented to certain dignitaries with jade. These are relics of the Han Dynasty and the Six Dynasties (from 2nd century B.C. to 6th century B.C.).

Understanding Jade

□ A woodcut print of Emperor Mu of the Zhou Dynasty being entertained by Xi Wang Mu at her palace on Kun Lun Mountains (note the famous eight horses of the emperor's carriage tethered at the bottom of the mountains).

JADE IN MYTHOLOGY 2

The Western Godmother and Kunlun Mountains

T he best known and popular myths of jade are *the palace of* Xi Wang Mu (西王母), *the Western Godmother* or Jin Mu (金母), *the Golden Mother*, set in the Kunlun Mountains, (崑崙山), a range dividing Tibet and Chinese Turkestan and regarded by geologists as the true backbone of the vast continent of Asia.

Xi Wang Mu's palace is in the Kunlun Mountains, with jade columns and balustrades. It is a jade palace with a lake of gems. Taoism has borrowed heavily from Hinduism, and from an early age Taoist mystics have identified Kunlun with Meru which is the Hindu's central mountain of the world around whose heaven-piercing summit revolved the sun, the moon and the stars. The myth of Kunlun Mountains is so important in Chinese mythology that it deserves more than just a mention. For over two thousand years the myth of this mountain range and the Western Godmother have provided the raw material and situations for numerous stories and folklore.

The marvels and delights of Kunlun appeared only after Confucius' time, and fabulists and dreamers alike vied with one another in their fantastic stories. A member of the imperial household of Han, Huai Nan Zi (淮南子), born 122 B.C., a dreamer and ardent Taoist, wrote this about Kunlun and the Western Godmother's palaces:

Understanding Jade

'It has walls piled high in the ninefold gradations, rising to the height of eleven thousand li (3 li = 1 mile); and upon it grow marvellous trees and grain. In the west, there are the tree of pearl, the trees of jade and other gems, and the tree of immortality; on the east . . . Weak water (弱水), on which nothing can float issues from a hollow rock and flows into the Moving Sands. (these are deserts with underground streams or sands moved violently by wind.)'

Xi Wang Mu is lovely beyond compare, but she could assume terrifying appearances – a being with a panther's tail and tiger's teeth and who howls loudly. Her hair hangs loose and she wears a coronet. She presides over the calamities and punishments sent by God. She is the leader of all the immortals who live on Kunlun where everything is made of jade or precious stones. The peach tree in her garden blooms every three thousand years and the fruits ripen in another three thousand years. Eating these peaches impart immortality.

These fantastic descriptions have given rise to even more fantastic stories in succeeding periods of Chinese history. At least two emperors are said to have met with Xi Wang Mu, Emperor Mu (穆王) of the Zhou dynasty 1001 B.C., as her guest on Kunlun, and Emperor Wu Di (武帝) of the Han dynasty 140 B.C., whom she visited in his palace. The stories of these royal friends of Xi Wang Mu and the lavish entertainment during their encounters have influenced and enriched Chinese art motifs and paintings. Numerous versions of these episodes have appeared in decorative art on porcelain plaques and vases, or simply in scroll paintings.

☐ *The qilin with a bundle of books in its mouth.*

Jade in Mythology

Confucius and the Jade Book

It is a Chinese belief that the muddy Yellow River clears once in 500 years or on the coming of an auspicious age or the birth of a great man. It is said that Confucius' mother became pregnant when she stepped on the footsteps of a *qilin* (麒麟) or celestial horse in the hills when she went to pray for a son. For this reason the *qilin* is sometimes depicted with the Goddess of Fecundity who has a child riding on her back. When Confucius was born not only did the muddy water of the Yellow River become clear, but the *qilin* appeared just before his birth at his house with a jade book in its mouth. The book had an inscription of ten words saying 'crystal child, continue with the decadent Zhou and onwards as thornless king' (水精之子，继衰周而素王). Confucius' mother was curious. She put this jade book in an embroidered pouch and tied it to the *qilin*'s horn, and the animal departed.

The *qilin* is sometimes translated as a unicorn, but it is not the same animal. It has the head of a dragon, the body of a deer with scales of a dragon, tail of an ox, and hoofs of a horse. It is one of the four spiritually endowed animals (四灵) according to the *Book of Rites* (周礼) written in the second millennium B.C. – the other three being the phoenix, dragon and tortoise. It is said that the *qilin* appeared again shortly before Confucius died, this time without the jade book. Since then it is believed that the *qilin* has never appeared again because mankind has degenerated and morals have decayed. The standard art motif of this fabulous animal is a single *qilin* with or without a book in its mouth, but never in pairs. This motif is used mostly in large murals facing an important building; like the mural of nine dragons in Beijing.

☐ *Drawing of the left piece of a pair of jade carvings with dragon and bird motifs - each is a mirror image of the other. From a book of drawings written by Wu Da Zhen.*

☐ *Another drawing from the same book showing a jade pendant with dragon motifs.*

Understanding Jade

□ A variation of the dragon motif used in jade carvings.

Jade in Alchemy and Medicine

Jade can confer immortality if taken in the right way, according to a book on alchemy by Bao Po Zi (枹朴子), also known as Ge Hong (葛洪) of the fourth century A.D., one of the most celebrated Taoists and practitioners of alchemy. According to this book, in the mineral kingdom, cinnabar, gold, silver and jade enjoy the highest repute as vitalized substances. Jade may be taken in either liquid or powdered form to attain immortality. However the side-effect of taking jade is fever. Constant consumption of jade will render the body 'light' and prolong life. Jade features prominently in the Chinese pharmacopoeia and its use is recorded in books on alchemy. As a medicine, its taste is neutral and its effect neither heaty nor cooling. It is supposed to eradicate shortness of breath and thirst as well as improve the health of the heart, liver, stomach, kidneys and lungs, the throat condition and voice whilst enriching the hair. Boiled with gold, silver and *Opheopogon japonicus* (麦冬), it is beneficial. Scars on the face or body are supposed to disappear if constantly rubbed with a piece of white jade. These and many other recipes with jade as an ingredient are contained in a monumental work of 52 books – *ben cao qang mu* (本草纲目) which took Li Shi Zhen (李时珍) of the Ming dynasty 30 years to compile. This standard monumental work is often referred to as the Chinese *Materia Medica* and is one of the main reference books of Chinese physicians. Whether the use of jade in alchemy and medicine is fact or fancy is difficult to ascertain, but I am quite certain that if jade is reduced to powder and taken in small quantities from time to time, it can do no harm, if not actually have beneficial effects.

Jade in Mythology

☐ A white jade disc (probably used as a button by a high official) with carvings of the hare pounding the elixir of immortality on the Moon, and the cockerel symbolising the Sun. These are two of the symbols that are on the Emperor's robes.

The Jade Hare (玉兔)

The legend of the Hare in the Moon is widely known in many countries, both in Europe and in Asia. In China the mention of the hare in legends appeared as early as the fourth century B.C. It is believed that the hare in Chinese legends must have come with Buddhism from India. The immortal Hare in the Moon pounds the herbs of immortality and appears luminous, hence the description Jade Hare (玉兔) The term has become synonymous with the moon. Since then the hare or rabbit has been an art motif in all mediums of Chinese art. Artists have painted the hare, craftsmen have created the hare in wood, porcelain, glass and most important of all in jade. This most loved animal in Chinese folklore is known to every Chinese. It stands for longevity, immortality, resurrection, peace, prosperity, and is an auspicious omen. The hare conceives by gazing at the Moon. It can live to a thousand years, and becomes white at 500 years from its natural brown (as opposed to the rabbit which is naturally white). Ancient Chinese writings have mentioned red hares and black hares. The Chinese generic term for both hare and rabbit is *tu*, and it appears quite obvious that the *tu* in Chinese mythology refers to the hare and not the rabbit which is more commonly white and therefore cannot again become white in 500 years. The hare pounding the herbs of immortality is one of the twelve symbols on the emperor's robes. It is used singly by high officials indicating their senior rank, either in the form of a jade button or simply embroidered on the robes.

Understanding Jade

The 'Most Precious Piece of Jade'

Some may look upon the piece of jade discovered by Bian He (卞和) of the State of Chu (楚) during the time of the Warring States in Chinese history, eighth century B.C. as part legend and part fact. The historical event and the person are real, but the jade is no longer in existence. Bian He discovered this piece of jade in Jing Mountains (荆山) in modern Hubei province (湖毛). There is a stone cave at the top said to be Bian He's living quarters and below that a cliff called Bao Yu Yan (抱玉岩) (meaning 'holding jade cliff') where Bian He is said to have found the jade. He hastened to present it to the King of Chu. Unfortunately the jade was declared ungenuine. For trying to deceive the king he was punished by amputation of his right foot. When the king was succeeded by another king, Bian He again tried to present his precious jade. Again it was rejected as a fake. This time he lost his left foot for trying to deceive the king a second time. When the third king came to the throne, Bian He had himself carried to the palace gate and he wept there. When he was asked by the king why he cried, he said it was not because he had lost both his feet, but because a precious piece of jade had been rejected by two kings as ungenuine and a loyal subject punished as a deceiver. The king thereupon called on the best lapidary of the land to examine the stone, and it was found to be the purest and most beautiful jade ever found. The jade was then named *he shi zhi bi* (和民之璧) after the discoverer Bian He, literally meaning 'Family He's jade tablet'. The king also wanted to make him a marquis, but he declined the honour. From this episode comes the proverbial expression 'Having eyes yet not recognising the jade of Jing Shan' (有眼不识荆山玉), meaning 'having eyes but blind to good things'. This precious piece of jade came into the possession of the State of Zhao (赵) during the turmoil of the Warring States and was much sought after by almost every state for a few hundred years. At one stage a state offered 15 cities in exchange for this piece of jade. At other times states went into battle for it. All these have been featured in the historical writings of the Warring States.

Prince Zhao of the State of Qin (秦昭王) 255 B.C., offered 15 of his cities to buy this precious jade from the State of Zhao (赵). The king of Zhao sent his emissary Lan Xiang Ru (蔺相如) with the jade to the State of Qin. After delivering the jade, Lan Xiang Ru discovered that the Prince of Qin had no intention of delivering the 15 cities to the State of Zhao. Lan then stole the jade and returned to his king, and was duly rewarded. One version says he threatened to smash the jade in front of the Prince of Qin when he discovered that the Prince had no intention of giving up his 15 cities. On seeing Lan's loyalty to his king and his bravery, the Prince of Qin called off the deal and

Lan returned with the jade intact. This incident in history has given birth to the idiomatic expression literally, 'The intact jade returns to Zhao' (完璧归赵), meaning 'a precious thing returns to its owner intact'.

'A Rainbow that Changed into a Jade Tablet'

It is said that when the 'Filial Piety Classic' (孝经) was completed, the author reported the fact to Heaven, whereupon a red rainbow in the sky changed into a tablet of yellow jade 3 feet long. 'The Filial Piety Classic' contains the conversation between Confucius and one of his disciples Zeng San (曾参) on filial piety, but the authorship is in doubt. Researchers indicate that it was probably written between the time of Mencius (372-289 B.C.) and the beginning of the Han dynasty 200 B.C. Some attributed the authorship to Mencius.

'The Jade Pin that Changed into a Swallow'

The legend goes thus: A fairy gave a jade hairpin to Emperor Han Wu Di (汉武帝), 140-86 B.C. The Emperor decided to give it to a lady friend whereupon the jealous court ladies conspired to destroy the hairpin. On opening the box they found that the jade hairpin had changed into a white swallow which duly flew away.

□ Jade ornament. Warring States period.

☐ *Jade plaque of Bodhidharma carved in relief and inscribed by a prime minister of the last Chinese dynasty.*

'The Jade Swallow'

The mother of Zhang Yue (张说), A.D. 667-730 of the Tang dynasty dreamed of a jade swallow entering her bosom, and gave birth to Zhang Yue. Zhang became one of the greatest scholars and statesmen of Tang and was made a duke.

'Fire Jade (火玉)'

The Tang dynasty was famous for subduing neighbouring countries, particularly east and west of China proper, which raided Chinese territory from time to time. During the reign of Tang Wu Chong (扶余国), A.D. 841-847, a subdued state Fu Yu Guo (唐武宗), which covered vast areas in modern eastern Manchuria, paid tribute to China with Fire Jade (火玉), which could keep a building warm in winter.

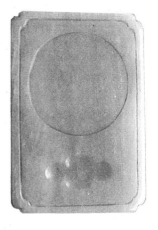

☐ *A pale green jade inkslab.*

Jade in Literature

Confucius said that superior men of old regarded jade as a symbol of virtues and that it was valuable for this reason. 'Its gentle, smooth and glossy appearance suggests clarity of heart; its fine texture and hardness suggest wisdom; its sharpness doing no injury suggests one's duty to one's neighbour; hanging down as if it would fall suggests righteousness; giving a clear note when struck symbolises music; its flaws not obscuring its beauties nor its beauties obscuring its flaws symbolise loyalty; its air of confidence symbolises heaven; its energy manifested in hills and streams symbolises earth; its chief place in articles of regalia of office symbolises excellence; and having under the sky nothing of equal value to it symbolises the Dao itself'. This statement of Confucius sums up the complete estimation of jade in Chinese civilization.

Understanding Jade

□ *Jade brush holder with brown incrustations carved as bark of a tree.*

It is not surprising therefore that in Chinese society the word jade is used to describe beautiful women or men as honorific. A beautiful woman is called *Yu Ren* (玉人), literally Jade Person; *Yu Shou* (玉手), literally Jade Hand, refers to the beautiful hand of a woman; and *Yu Sun* (玉筍), literally Jade Bamboo Shoot, refers to the beautiful fingers of women. Generally as an honorific it is used in *Yu Ti* (玉体), precious body; *Yu Zhi* (玉趾), precious footsteps; *Yu Rong* (玉容), precious face etc. Even the Chinese version of God Almighty is called *Yu Di* (玉帝), Jade Emperor, who rules Heaven and is the Taoist equivalent of God in Heaven. He is by far the most popular of all Chinese Gods. His birthday falls on the 9th day of the first moon in the lunar year, and is celebrated far and wide. In some places, the Jade Emperor is worshipped as the Ancestor of Jade.

In ancient times when the roles of men and women were clearly divided in a society that was male orientated, giving birth to a boy was *long zhang* (弄璋), literally 'playing with the jade tablet zhang'. It is a fact that the child was given a jade tablet to play with so that he would grow up with the qualities and virtues of jade. Today the literary term *long zhang* has come to mean: giving birth to a boy. Girls were given a piece of pottery to play with at birth, which was in fact part of the spindle made of pottery to hold the silk. Giving birth to a girl is therefore *nong wa* (弄瓦), literally 'playing with pottery', so that the girl will grow up knowing how to spin well. There is nothing superior or inferior between these two expressions, as some social critics would say. It was merely a custom at the time when boys and girls were brought up to perform their respective roles in life in a tightly structured society. However, in spite of the social changes today, these literary expressions have come to stay.

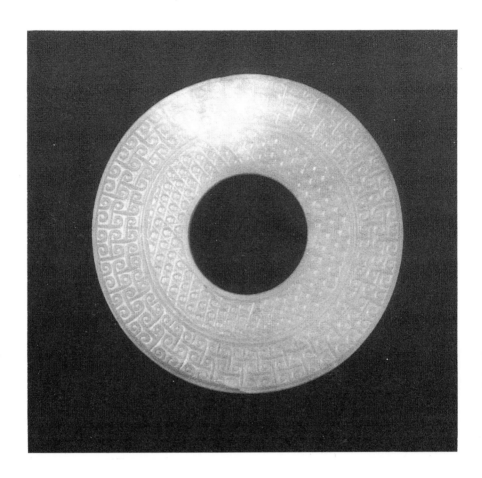

White jade disc.

JADE AND ITS QUALITIES 3

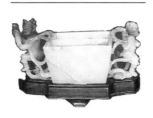

Identification of Jade

T his is an important but perhaps the most difficult part in the study and enjoyment of jade. Not every person has the facilities to identify jade through scientific processes which would rely on factors such as hardness, specific gravity and temperature of fusion. Such a procedure is used for scientific purposes and not by persons whose object is to acquire a piece of jade for aesthetic reasons. To many beginners, indeed even experienced persons, the rule of thumb is to try and scratch the jade with a steel point, such as the tip of a penknife. If it remains unscratched, then chances are that the piece is genuine. This eliminates those stones which are softer than jade. The average steel point has a hardness of less than 6 mohs and will not scratch either nephrite or jadeite. This method is not conclusive. The rest depends on knowledge of texture and colour. Jade is usually translucent and can be even opaque if it is a low quality stone which contains impurities.

Reading about jade provides basic knowledge about jade but identifying jade accurately requires more than what you can learn from a book. The only way to learn to identify jade is through constant handling. There is no short cut to this knowledge. A trained or experienced eye will be able to identify jade through sight and touch. Scratching a piece of jade with a penknife is not the ultimate test. It is just an approximate test to eliminate stones which are not jade because they are softer and can be scratched; especially soapstone

Understanding Jade

☐ *Cross-section of a piece of raw jade with the crusty brown outer layer still intact.*

which can be polished to look like jade. There are a great many semi-precious stones with a degree of hardness equal to or higher than jade such as quartz, agate and serpentine. To the experienced eye these other semi-precious stones have different textures and appearances from jade. For example, quartz has many fractures in the crystal; serpentine is translucent and flawless whilst having a pale green colour. The descriptions of jade in this book can help the reader identify the stone by exposing him to as much information as the scope of the book offers but there is no substitute for first-hand encounters with jade. Many a collector has learnt his/her hobby the hard and expensive way. Perhaps what is more important to collectors is that they are happy with their collection as it is more of a manifestation of their personal satisfaction in their taste and aesthetic sense than anything else.

What is Good Jade?

This is often a difficult question to answer. It depends on whether you are referring to ancient jade, modern jade, ornamental objects or jewellery. Jade is translucent and not transparent like glass. Opacity lowers its quality. Cracks and presence of impurities further reduce its value. However the beauty of a piece of jade will be enhanced if there is a small flaw somewhere, just as, it is said, a gentleman with a little fault is more interesting than one without.

The most important determinant of the quality of jade is colour. Generally people identify green and white with jade although, as I have stated earlier, there are many colours in jade depending on the minerals present in it. Throughout Chinese history writers have written treatises on jade, especially during the last four to five hundred years, and they have put different emphases on the colours. Some say red jade is the best, followed by white, yellow and black. Green with the colour of dead vegetable leaves is the lowest grade. Some say bright green is the best, the deeper the green the better, followed by mutton fat white, red and so on. In fact if one has the chance to read all the treatises, one will realise that there are as many classifications as there are colours. In my view, so long as it is either nephrite or jadeite and the translucency is right with few flaws, the colour is really a matter of personal taste, especially in items of jewellery.

Carved objects and figurines could be of any colour, depending on what they are. Usually white jade is used for carving objects, although it is not uncommon to find the most colourful jade carved into an art object which it is the intention of the craftsman to represent. For instance there are extant 'jade' cabbages with all the natural colours of the real thing, whole landscapes carved out of jade with green trees, brown rocks and blue hills, or figurines with the natural colours of flesh and clothings. Indeed jade craftsmen with magic eyes and divine tools have not been in short supply in this field throughout Chinese history.

☐ A white jade cup.

Understanding Jade

□ *White jade ewer shaped after the Bronze Age ewers. The black spots enhance the beauty of the jade piece.*

Old and New Jade

There are standard Chinese terms for naming old and new jade, such as *gu* 古, *jin* 今, *xin* 新, and *jiu* 旧, meaning 'ancient', 'modern' or contemporary, 'new' and 'old' respectively. New jade, as the name implies, is newly crafted jade. Ancient jade is divided into two types: that which has been buried and that which has not been buried. Jade from ancient times which has not been buried is called *Zhuan Shi Gu* (传世古), literally 'handed down the generations'. Those which have been buried and recovered again are called *jiu yu* (旧玉), literally 'old jade'.

Jade & Its Qualities

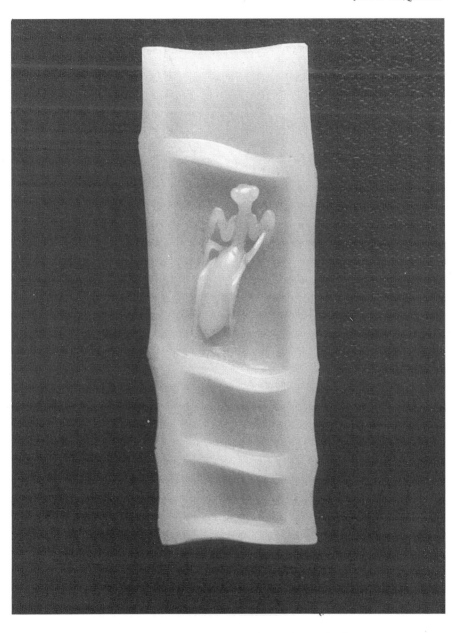

☐ *The inner section of a piece of white jade carved into a bamboo showing a praying mantis. The other half (not shown) is carved to fit exactly with this piece.*

Understanding Jade

□ 2 pieces of ancient jade worn on official's garments.
Left: a girdle pendant
Right: a cap button

There is another type of old jade called *han yu* (琀玉). It literally means 'jade put in the mouth of a dead person', which is generally burial jade used in stuffing a dead person's orifices. The piece on the tongue is shaped like a cicada which goes well with the tongue, and the others are shaped accordingly to suit the various orifices of the human body. Many people have mistakenly called 'old jade' Han Yu, perhaps confusing the jade of the Han dynasty with burial jade. The word Han for Han dynasty is 汉 which is different from the Han 琀 of burial jade. The 'han' of Han dynasty and the 'han' of Han Yu have the same romanised spelling, but are actually two different Chinese characters. Herein lies the difficulty in using romanized Chinese: as they are based on sound, confusion invariably arises because two characters can sound similar yet mean entirely different things. Even a Chinese speaker finds it difficult to differentiate the number of tones, especially in the dialects, although the two main tones, level ' 平 ' and oblique ' 仄 ' are common to all.

Modern jade is different from new jade in that it is older than newly crafted pieces. Perhaps we can say that it has been in existence for more than a hundred or more years but here we run into difficulties with the question: 'how many more years over a hundred?' Here we must look at the age of ancient jade. The standard periods of change in the colouring of buried jade are:

(1) Five hundred years when it becomes penetrable to foreign matter which will induce a change in colour;
(2) One thousand years when it becomes stony and dull;
(3) Two thousand years when it assumes the appearance of bones – opaque in colour ;
(4) In Three thousand years it becomes soft; and
(5) In Six thousand years, it disintegrates.

It is therefore safe to say that jade which is less than five hundred years old can be called 'modern jade'. Considering the long history of China, five hundred years is not a very long time. Five hundred years is also the length of time required for ancient jade to change colour if it is buried. Though the standard periods of change in the colour of buried jade are commonly recognised in the identification of old jade, in practice the period of change must depend on the condition of the soil. Dampness, presence of acids and heat have the effect of accelerating the change.

□ *Jade ornament. Warring States period.*

Understanding Jade

Colour Change

Pure jade is white, but the presence of other minerals in the jade gives it different colours. For example, the presence of iron gives it a green colour; chromium makes it black; and if the soil is acidic the salts of these minerals can give the jade a large variety of shades and mixture of colours. Buried jade, which is already crafted and has no outer crust for protection, undergoes more extensive colour change. Connoisseurs prize buried jades highly because these pieces, especially after being held by human hands for some time, undergo further changes. They become waxy and more shiny; the colour becomes brighter and more intense. Even a piece of buried jade which has become opaque as a result of a long burial period can become clearer and regain its translucency if handled by human hands or kept close to the warmth of the human body for many years. This type of jade is called *Tuo Tai Yu*, literally meaning 'reborn jade', and is very much sought after by collectors of ancient jade. One important point to remember when handling ancient jade is to avoid contaminating the jade with oily substances. Once the oil penetrates the cracks or weak veins in the jade which has already been penetrated by minerals in the earth during burial, no amount of touch or fondling will bring back its lustre.

□ *A white jade bracelet, partially disintegrated due to a long burial period. Carved with the ancient dragon motif, circa Warring States 3rd century B.C.*

Jade & Its Qualities

Faking Jade

Like everything else jade can be faked, both modern and ancient. With the advance of technology many things can be faked and passed off as the real thing. Outside of scientific processes, a piece of stone can be passed off as ancient jade because of the stone's 'dead' texture and colour which gives it the appearance of jade buried for a long time. A piece of stone containing jade can be made to look like ancient jade if it is roasted in red wood sawdust or black wood sawdust to make it red or black at the cracks or weak veins and then passed off as buried jade.

Just as new bronze can be buried in the ground and have urine poured over it daily for some months or a year to develop a beautiful patina in order to pass it off as ancient bronze, jade can be treated to acquire an ancient appearance. It is said that if a dog is killed without letting out blood and the jade is buried in its stomach while the dog's body is still warm, and the whole carcass is buried in the ground for a few years, the jade will acquire a blood-red appearance with varying patterns of marking depending on the texture. To the unwary or untrained eye this is ancient jade. To the expert the colour has no depth and there may be other tell-tale marks, just like the patina on the urine-treated bronze which has no depth. Jade boiled in acidic solutions such as vinegar or black plum juice, and suddenly taken out and exposed to extreme cold, such as snow or ice, will have fine hair cracks which can be treated with colour to give it a 'buried' look. Such jade, after some time, will lose its colour and expose itself as having been 'doctored'. Constant handling or boiling in water will accelerate its loss of colour. And if jade is burned it produces a dull bone-like appearance which is like that of ancient jade.

☐ *A pale green bracelet, discoloured through burial with the dead.*

Why do craftsmen as well as others fake jade? Fakes exist as part of the world of art and antiques. As long as there is a profitable market for art like porcelain, bronzes, paintings, etc, there will always be fakes. In the case of jade, one can either fake jade with other less valuable stones as substitutes for the real thing, or use new jade and treat it to look like ancient jade. Even trademarks are subject to this practice.

However, I am certain that in ancient times, craftsmen copied the older objects because their style was beautiful. In the renaissance of the Ming Dynasty, there was a re-emphasis on the classic forms of art. After the Mongol yoke was thrown off, the Ming Dynasty brought fresh and renewed interest in Chinese history, scholarship and art. Many monochrome porcelain pieces were produced in the style of the Song monochromes. Bronze vessels and other art objects followed the ancient forms of Han and earlier dynasties. Even literary writings of poetry and prose acquired a new style and flavour akin to the Song and Tang era. Indeed the Ming Dynasty was a great period in the revival of Chinese art and scholarship.

When foreigners started to arrive in China in greater numbers during the Ming and Qing (Manchu) dynasties, a profitable and sizeable market was set up in the Chinese antique trade. Early copies which were innocently copied as ancient pieces found a ready market amongst both foreign and Chinese collectors. This practice still exists today, if not with greater veracity as the demand for antiques has caught on so quickly and so extensively.

Distinguishing a fake or copy from a genuine piece is no easy task. Short of using chemical or other scientific tests, this will depend on the experience, knowledge and judgement of the potential jade buyer. Even experts do not or cannot collude in their opinions of what is real and what is fake. Much as collectors and connoisseurs will depend on expert advice or their own judgement, sizing up a jade piece remains essentially a subjective and personal practice. If a collector believes that the piece is genuine and buys it, it will remain so for him – there is no authority that dictates otherwise!

All Jade Pieces can be Carried

Apart from ancient pieces which were meant to be carried as pendants, this practice of carrying jade for protection has extended to all art objects which are small enough to be carried as pendants or merely in the pocket, or as multi-purpose fingering jade – in one instance being fondled in the hand, the next hung from the girdle and finally nestled in the pocket. There is no limit in the enjoyment of jade.

Enjoyment of Jade

Music can only be enjoyed if it is played, or else the piece of written music is 'dead' after the composer has written it. A painting after completion is there to be looked at and appreciated but not touched. Most people who are untutored like to touch a Chinese painting. This is one of the most important *don'ts* in looking at a painting. The finger may be oily or dirty or the painting may be so old that it is fragile and may be damaged. In the case of jade, not to touch the jade is to miss the whole essence of the artistic enjoyment of jade. The joy of the softness of touch of jade, which is described as *jun* (润) cannot be explained in words. It can only be experienced. The visual delights of looking at the beautiful colouration and delicate carving of jade cannot match the delights of the sensitive touch of jade.

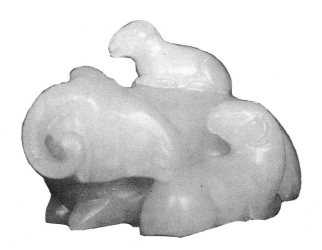

□ *A carving showing three lambs in white jade.*

Understanding Jade

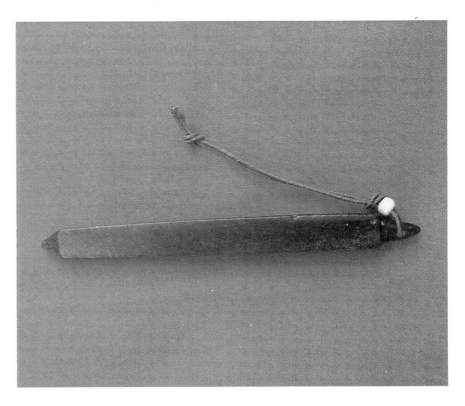

☐ A jade amulet used in ancient times as a decoration for the ear. It was also used as burial jade: one of those used to stuff the orifices of the body. This is for stuffing the ear, called 'zhen'.

HISTORICAL JADE   4

It is said that stone implements of the Stone Age merge into jade implements of the Jade Age, and the jade tablet *gui* is modelled after the stone axe-head of the Stone Age. Generally it is believed that in Chinese civilization, stone implements were used during the reign of Emperor Shennong (神农), around 2737 B.C.; jade was used during the reign of the Yellow Emperor Huang Di (黄帝) , around 2697 B.C.; bronze was used during the reign of Emperor Yu 禹 , around 2205 B.C. and the Iron Age dawned at the end of the Zhou dynasty, 1122 – 255 B.C. At one stage it was doubted whether the Stone Age actually existed in China, until stone implements were dug up from graves of the Zhou dynasty in the northern provinces of China along the Yellow River Basin, which is the cradle of Chinese civilization. The use of jade in religion and ceremonial rites is recorded in some of the earliest books such as the *Zhou Li* (周礼), the *Li Ji* (礼记), which are all books of rites, and the *Shi Jing* (诗经), or *Book of Poetry*. The *Book of Poetry* 'sings' the virtues and the beauties of this precious stone.

Throughout the ages to the present jade has been sung about in poems and immortalised as the most exquisite of all precious things. Li Po has compared jade with love – the older the more valuable.

There is no doubt that jade was used by the emperors in ancient ceremonies because of its preciousness and beauty. Then it became the material for social uses and ornamentation, first by sovereigns and dignitaries and later by the common people. Writers and researchers who have made studies into this subject have classified the use of jade through the ages in many ways. I find a simple broad classification into ceremonial uses and social uses the easiest and most logical.

Understanding Jade

☐ *An old print of a craftsman cutting jade with a toothless circular saw powered by a foot pedal.*

Jade 'Carving'

Jade 'carving' consists of first cutting a large piece of jade into smaller pieces using a toothless saw which has sand or grit applied to its edge. This sand should be harder than jade. The stone is shaped approximately to the size and shape of the intended object by a process whereby the unwanted portions and corners are ground away by the grit of hard stones. With the advance of technology today, carborundum is used which has a hardness of 9 mohs, close to that of diamond which is a 10. A turning lathe or drill is used powered by a foot pedal. This method is still used and is thousands of years old. All that has changed are the electric driven lathes and drills to make things more efficient. By and large the process remains the same from cutting to polishing. Now tin oxide is used instead of the old goat skin or skin of dry gourd as the final polishing agent. This final polishing stage is most important as the colour and finish of the stone are determined by this. The jade that is described are fine examples of the craftsmanship of the artists and artisans who have produced the jade with this process.

The *Gui* (圭)

Among ancient jade objects the most important were the ceremonial jade tablets called *gui* (圭). There were two groups of such tablets – six of one and six of the other.

The six used by the emperor and other dignitaries were called *liu jui* (六瑞) : *zhen gui* (镇圭) for emperor, *heng gui* (桓圭) for a duke (公), *xin gui* (信圭) for a marquis (侯), *gong gui* (躬圭) for an earl (伯), *gu bi* (谷璧) for a viscount (子), *pu pi* (蒲璧) for a baron (男). These were all symbols of authority, and the *gui* were of the same shape but differed in size. Similarly the *bi* had the same shape but had different decorative motifs.

The other six were used solely by the emperor for the worshipping of Heaven and Earth and the Four directions. They were called *liu qi* (六器). The *zhang bi* (苍璧), jade disc for worshipping Heaven, *huang cong* (黄琮) a yellow jade cylinder for worshipping Earth, *qing gui* (青圭) a blue tablet for worshipping the East, *chi zhang* (赤璋) a red tablet for the South, *bai fu* (白琥) a white jade tiger for the West, and *xuan huang* (玄璜) a black crescent for the North. These *gui* and *bi* were the earliest objects used in ceremonies, and the *gui* were shaped after the early stone axe-heads. Although

Understanding Jade

the *liu jui* and the *liu qi* were of definite sizes and patterns, there were large numbers of *gui* and *bi* made of different sizes and patterns for less important uses.

☐ *Drawings of various types of gui — they vary from a few inches in length to three feet. Note the axe-head at the extreme top right and the tablet which symbolises power.*

Historical Jade

The Cong (琮)

Various theories have been put forward by researchers and scholars on the purpose of this strangely shaped jade object, a sort of square tube with a round hole through it. The outer surface can be plain or carved with designs, mainly lines or other geometric designs. The size of this object varies from a few inches to about 8 or more inches. The jade is fairly thick and may be of any colour, but mainly yellow, russet or red. All research point to the *cong* as an object used for worshipping the earth because of its shape. While the *bi* was used for the worship of Heaven, it was considered logical that the *cong* was used for worshipping the Earth. Sometimes the shape of the *cong* is not exactly square. The four corners are rounded off and the shape is more eight-sided than square. The *cong* could also be considered to be a symbol of the Universe – Heaven is round and the Earth is square, hence the *cong* is square on the outside and round on the inside.

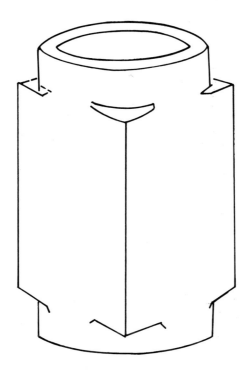

□ *A characteristic cong*

Understanding Jade

Burial Jade

From recorded writings of the Zhou dynasty, second millennium B.C., many objects which were said to be used for ceremonial purposes, were also used for burial of the dead. The following objects were laid with the dead for burial: *gui* (圭) on the left of the corpse, *zhang* (璋) at the head, *fu* (琥) on the right, *huang* (璜) at the feet, *bi* (璧) on the back, and *cong* (琮) on the stomach. Although these positions have been recorded as the points of placement of these jade objects on the corpse, so far no corpse has been discovered with these jade objects in the places stated, except the *bi* which has been found on the chest or back of corpses in ancient tombs. Nevertheless it is safe to assume that these early jade objects were used for religious or ceremonial, including burial, purposes. There were other minor jade articles used for burial in addition to these larger ones, such as the jade cicada and other articles suitably shaped to fit the nine orifices (九窍) of the human body. Those used for stuffing the orifices were called *zhen* (瑱).

The nine orifices are divided into two groups – the 7 Yang orifices (阳窍) comprising the eyes, ears, nose and mouth, and the 2 Ying orifices (阴窍) comprising the anus and the sex organ. It is believed that the stuffing of these 9 orifices with jade will preserve the corpse from disintegrating.

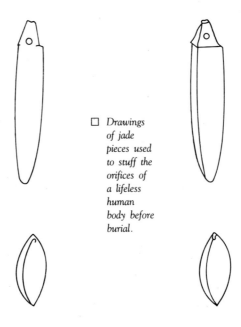

□ *Drawings of jade pieces used to stuff the orifices of a lifeless human body before burial.*

Historical Jade

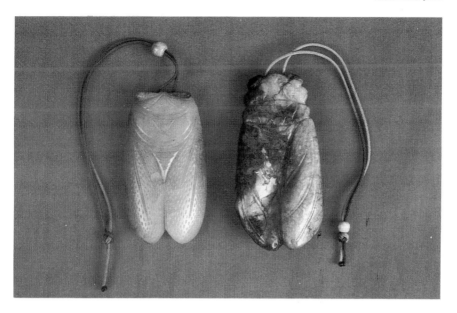

□ 2 white jade cicadas, one somewhat damaged as a result of long burial in the ground.

The Cicada (蝉)

The cicada is a symbol of resurrection and is the most popular object used for burial. It is put on the tongue and it fits nicely because of its shape. It is shaped simply to symbolise the cicada or sometimes more elaborately carved with details of wings, eyes and other body lines. From excavations of ancient tombs the cicada appears to have been widely used during the Zhou and the Han dynasties. Because of its life history, the cicada is perceived as a symbol of resurrection. The larva works its way into the earth, and, after a long subterranean existence of many years, emerges to the surface in the pupa stage from which it is transformed into the cicada. The cicada had appeared on bronze vessels as an art form long before it was carved in jade for the dead.

51

Understanding Jade

The Jade Pig (玉豚)

This is one of the rare jade objects found in ancient China. It is a stylised jade pig, the purpose of which has not been clearly ascertained. It has been found in tombs of the Han period both in Korea and North China, and from a study of its position in relation to the corpse in the coffin, it would appear to have been put in the armpit of the corpse.

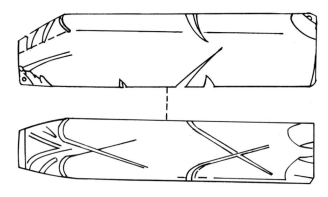

☐ *Drawings of a jade pig found in ancient graves.*

The Weng Zhong (翁仲)

This is a very interesting and strongly stylised human figure varying from a couple of inches to 6 inches. This figure's beauty lies in its simplicity, and the whole figure is made up of just four triangles – the head, the two sleeves and the bottom half. The name of the figurines suggests that it must have originated from the time of the Builder of the Great Wall of China, Qin Shi Huang (秦始皇), third century B.C. It has the name of Qin Shi Huang's special guard measuring 13 feet in height for whom a statue was erected after his death. From very early times this figure has been cast in bronze and iron, and also carved in stone. Although it is not burial jade, it has been found in some ancient tombs together with the jade objects.

Historical Jade

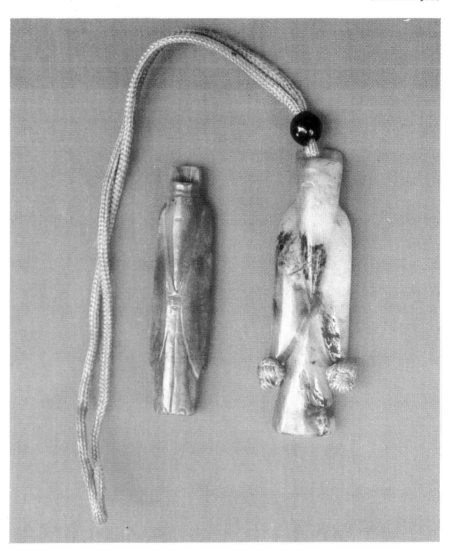

☐ Weng Zhong (probably Han dynasty)
left: Deep brown jade   right: White jade, discoloured by burial.

Understanding Jade

Tallies *Fu* (符)

These tallies were originally shaped like the *gui* and in fact the five of them were called *zhen gui* (珍圭), *yan gui* (琰圭), *yuan gui* (琬圭), *gu gui* (谷圭), and *ya zhang* (牙璋).

All these tallies were used to send out orders of all types from military to social businesses for rewards and punishments. They were later (sixth century B.C.) replaced by Tiger Tallies *Hu Fu* (虎符) which were more elaborately carved into the shape of a tiger, and some were split into 2 halves to facilitate identification by fitting the 2 halves into one. This change made imitation of the tallies difficult. In some tallies, the 2 halves had one single word carved into each, one in raised relief and the other grooved so that only the correct pieces will fit properly.

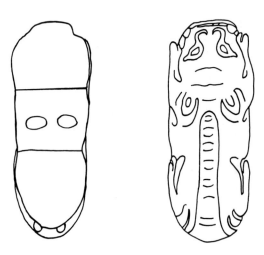

☐ *Outline drawing of an actual military tally in the shape of a tiger of Han dynasty (plan and underside of tally)*

Historical Jade

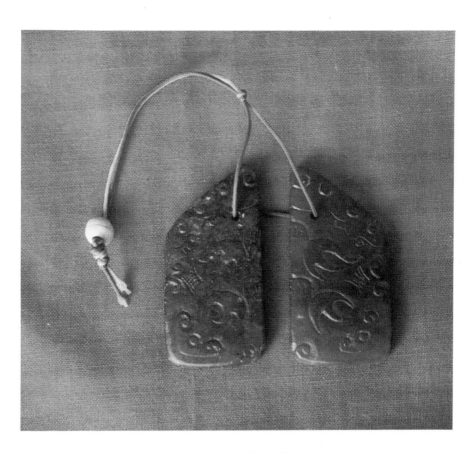

☐ *A pair of military tallies.*

☐ Jade carving of a gourd

Historical Jade

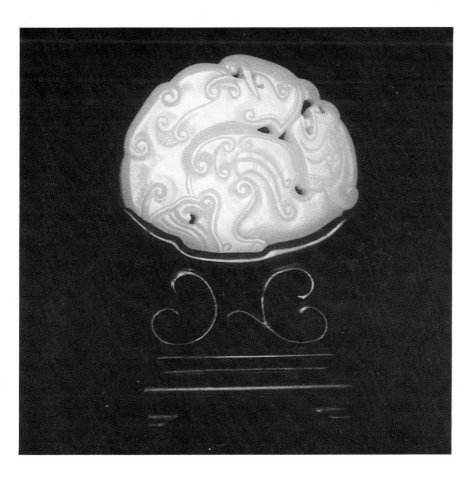

☐ White jade pendant of the dragon and the phoenix.

☐ *White jade pendant of five bats symbolising the five blessings of life — longevity, health, wealth, plenty of progeny and blessing.*

JADE AND MORTALS   5

We have seen how jade was used originally in Chinese civilization for spiritual or religious purposes, and as symbols of authority and power. It even acquired a mystic character as something that could be in communion with the universe. Its use was confined to 'big' men such as emperors, high officials and 'superior men', that is, men of character and status. Gradually the uses of jade were expanded. Instead of using jade carved symbolically for sacrificial matters, such as the *gui*, the *cong* and other symbols described in the previous chapters, jade objects were carved in the shapes of ancient bronze vessels, cups and other objects of utility. Not only were the objects copies of the more ancient bronzes, but the designs on their surfaces were also copies. Jade seals which were known to have been in use in Zhou times, came into prominence in Qin (255-209 B.C.) and Han (206 B.C.-A.D. 189) times. During these two dynasties only emperors and other royalty were allowed to use jade seals. Others used stone, pottery, wood, bamboo or other materials for their seals.

It is said that when Qin Shi Huang, Builder of the Great Wall of China, finally conquered the six Warring States in 221 B.C. and unified China, he set up his Qin empire and proclaimed himself Emperor. Qin Shi Huang means the first emperor of Qin. He had hoped that his descendants would be second emperor of Qin, third emperor of Qin and so on ad infinitum. Those were wild hopes and ambitions, and his empire collapsed in the reign of his son, the second emperor (秦二世) in 209 B.C. Qin was conquered by Liu Bang

Understanding Jade

☐ *The legendary jade seal of the Builder of the Great Wall, Chin Shih Huang, carved out of the most precious piece of jade discovered by Bian He, said to be lost at the end of the Song Dynasty. The characters in 'bird' form symbolise Chin Shih Huang communicating with Heaven. The eight words （ 受命於天，旣壽永昌 ）
mean 'Mandate from Heaven, Longevity and Everlasting Prosperity'.*

(刘邦) who set up the Han dynasty (206 B.C. to A.D. 189). When Qin subdued the six Warring States, 'the most precious jade' discovered by Bian He, which had become the property of the State of Zhao and for which Qin had earlier offered 15 cities to acquire it, was surrendered to Qin. It was carved into a seal for the Qin emperor. For the first time this Imperial Seal was called the 'Country Succession Seal' (传国玺). It is said that it became the property of the emperors of succeeding dynasties that ruled China, but the seal perished with the demise of the Song dynasty (A.D. 960-1278) when the last emperor died in a shipwreck near Ya Shan off the Guandong coast trying to escape the Mongol invaders. This famous seal is said to have been carved out of *he shi zhi pi* (family He's jade tablet) which must be lying at the bottom of the sea off the southern coast of Guangdong, China, near the island of Ya Shan, not far from Macao. Perhaps some adventurous salvaging company may try to salvage the piece along with other treasures.

Another Famous Jade Seal

The seal of pure white jade of Han Cheng Di's (汉成帝) consort, 38-32 B.C., is one of very famous seals still extant until the Japanese invasion of China in the 1930s. It was in a collection of seven to eight thousand seals of the Han dynasty belonging to a very wealthy Chinese official who lived during the middle of the 19th century. Facsimiles of the seals in this collection were published in 1925 by the Commercial Press of Shanghai, but the publication is no longer available. This seal of the royal consort, who later became empress, and empress dowager after the emperor's death, is of great historical interest. Her name was Zhao Fei Yan (赵飞燕), Fei Yan meaning 'flying swallow', because of her light body and great dancing talents. The seal is of mutton fat jade, only one inch square and half an inch thick with the top carved in the shape of a flying swallow. The four words *jie yu qie zhao* (婕仔妾赵) designate her official rank and family name of Zhao. The style of the characters is of the Qin dynasty seal form.

□ *The jade seal of Zhao Fei Yan*

Understanding Jade

☐ White jade pendant of a dragon protecting a baby dragon inside.

☐ Bronze coin during the reign of Cheng-te. The symbols of his reign are shown here whilst the other side has the symbol of the dragon and phoenix together. This is a much copied design for jade coins.

Jade & Mortals

☐ *White jade pendants carved in relief. The first showing a young boy holding a pomegranate and the second showing a portrait of a lady.*

Pendants, *Pei*

Apart from large jade objects, there are numerous smaller ones which can be kept close to the human body as pendants or *pei* (佩). It is believed that jade, being a living stone, likes the warmth of the human body. The closer and longer it is in contact with human warmth, the more lustrous it becomes. Its lustre is an indicator of the state of health of the person with whom it is in constant contact. The benefit or advantage to both jade and man is mutual. Man is protected by the jade he wears or carries (apart from the old tradition that 'Gentlemen carry jade' to acquire the virtues of jade, described by Confucius and to remind themselves that they must not be rash, 君子佩玉以自宽). In ancient times the pieces of jade carried were mainly pendants which were hung from the girdle or in conjunction with a tassel. Fingering jades, which can be fondled in the hands, came into vogue later in history, particularly in the last few centuries.

Understanding Jade

The Gang Mao (刚卯)

This jade pendant, which looks like a seal, is an ancient and interesting pendant which men carried for protection against evil spirits. It originated during the time of the usurper Wang Mang (王莽) of the Han throne, 9 B.C. It is a small 3-inch long rectangular piece of jade with a 1-inch square cross-section which has a hole through the square end to enable a cord to be put through it so that it can be carried. Each of the four rectangular faces has 8 characters carved in two rows of 4 characters each. Smaller pieces can be as small as 1 inch in height with a half-inch square cross-section. Most of the words carved indicate that they are to ward off evil spirits. These pendants are carved only on the days in the first moon of the Lunar Year corresponding to the earthly branch Mao (卯), and on no other day Many of these pendants are still extant today. There are also gold and peach stone Gang Mao.

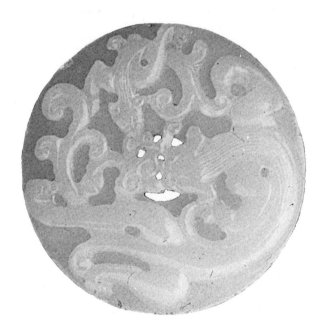

☐ A jade pendant with dragon design.

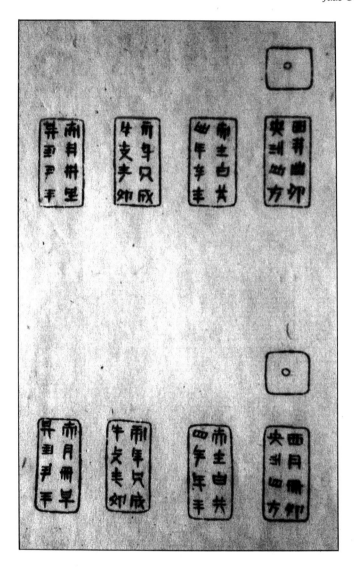

□ *Drawings of Gang Mao pendants.*

Understanding Jade

Military Tallies (琥符)

Original military tallies or their copies are also favourite pieces carried as pendants or fingering jade to ward off evil spirits because of the symbolic tiger. They may be single pieces or in pairs.

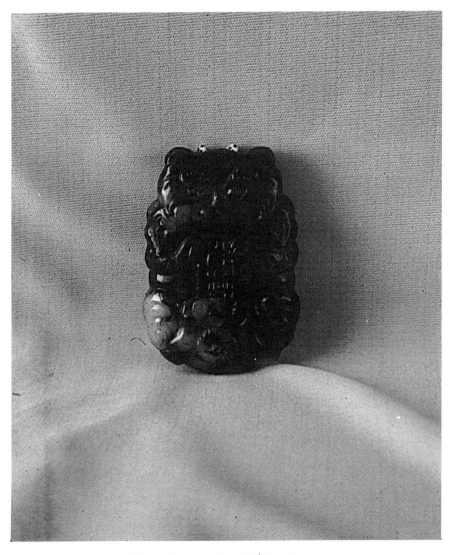

☐ *Military tally in the shape of the Han dynasty tiger.*

☐ *Green jade pendant.*

☐ Jade pendant with a pair of love birds carved in relief.

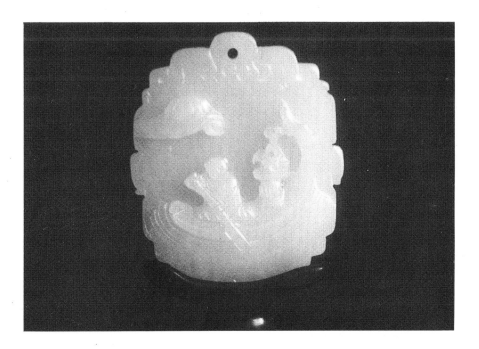

☐ White jade pendant of one of the Eight Immortals carved in relief.

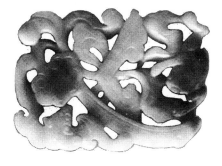

☐ An intricately carved design of a jade pendant.

Understanding Jade

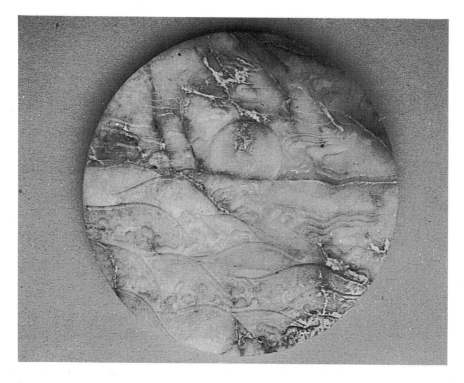

□ *A jade disc showing the one-legged bird in the sun over the waves.*

JADE AS ORNAMENT AND ART 6

The Jade Hairpin *Ji* (笄)

This is probably the earliest jade ornament in Chinese civilization, a hairpin to do up the hair of a girl when she reached the age of 15. The structure of the character *ji* has a bamboo radical, which suggests that this hairpin must have been originally made of bamboo. By the time the *Book of Rites* was written in the second millennium B.C., and other rules of ceremony and etiquette were established, it became the rule that a girl at 15 should have her hair done up and fixed with a hairpin, and at 20 she should marry – 十五而笄, 二十而嫁。 Jade was already in use at the time and the jade hairpin was in common use among the well-to-do. A young man would similarly be capped at the age of 20 and marry at 30 – 二十而冠, 三十而立。

Doing up the hair of girls and the capping of young men when they come of age in the second millennium B.C. was practically universal among the Chinese right through the ages. This practice was even transplanted to areas where the Chinese have migrated. Until very recently Chinese in Penang and Malacca followed this tradition with some modification in that the girl and the young man would undergo this ceremony only on the eve of their marriage, but not before. Whether ancient or modern, the ceremony is a symbol of the girl and the young man coming of age or reaching adulthood.

Understanding Jade

□ Green jade buckle.

Jade As Ornament & Art

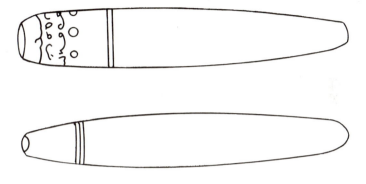

□ *Drawing of a jade hairpin used in ancient times.*

Jewellery

Jade, being the stone par excellence, is obviously a favourite material used for jewellery, apart from other precious or semi-precious stones, gold and other metals. Jade has the advantage over other stones because of its special texture and touch, colour, and the power (which the Chinese believe) to protect the person who carries it. Whether you believe it or not, it does not matter, if you only wish to appreciate its colour and touch. Many incidents have been reported and known to me personally where a person has escaped unscathed falling down a staircase or into a drain, in an accident, or other near-tragic circumstances because he or she had a piece of jade on the person. In some cases the piece of jade broke, leaving the person unharmed. I personally had the experience of a near-tragic car skid and spin on a Malaysian trunk road many years ago. My car suddenly skidded and spun for some 50 yards and ended travelling forward in the opposite direction, then for no apparent reason, it travelled backwards and landed with its back wheels in a shallow ditch. All that was required was to get assistance to pull the car up, and I continued the

Understanding Jade

☐ *A necklace of jade beads.*

journey without further mishaps. It is frightening to think of it now. At the time I had no idea why or how it could have happened and how the car missed all the traffic on the road. Only after many days did I realise that my car-key was attached to a jade ring and I had a piece of fingering jade in my pocket. I have been carrying a piece of fingering jade in the pocket wherever I go for some 50 years. I am not a superstitious person. The purpose is to fondle it and improve its smoothness and lustre; and, in flying especially, if the pilot should land his plane more abruptly, it feels good to have the jade in my hand to squeeze hard to increase courage and reduce the tension. No words can actually describe this feeling. You have to experience it. The jade ring to hold the car-key is nothing more than to have a good feel whenever you handle the key and to ensure the key is not easily lost. Of course, the incident could be just luck.

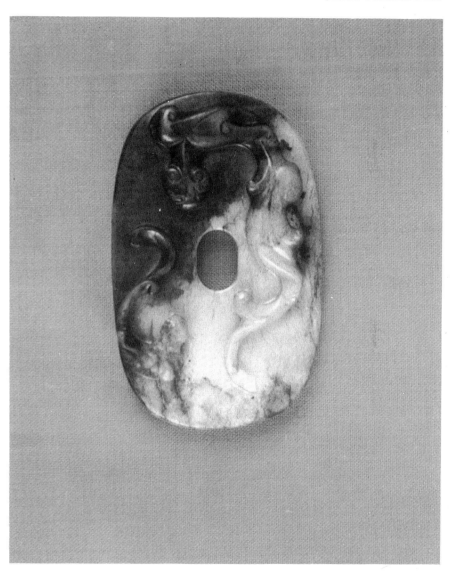

☐ An old jade piece with carvings of dragons in relief in an interesting shape.

Personal Jewellery

Personal jewellery includes rings, ear-rings, bracelets or bangles, necklaces, hairpins, and pendants. All these articles of course have different styles in design and qualities depending on the wealth and taste of the person concerned. Women obviously wore more types of jade whereas men in most cases would have only a jade ring. Some men in the past (this is hardly seen nowadays) wore jade bangles, especially bangles which had been buried with the dead and already discoloured. The beauty of these bangles lies in their colour and discolouration which remains dull after recovery from the earth but will become lustrous after years of contact with the human body again. The wearer can enjoy the experience of the change over a period of time.

☐ Jade necklace.

Women are less inclined to wear burial jade because of its initial dullness in colour. They prefer 'fresh' jade, green and colourful, lustrous and shining. It gives them a sense of well-being, which would add to their poise and grace. Invariably a piece of jade is set in gold, silver or platinum either singly or together with other precious stones. If the jade is by itself a 'showpiece' of very high quality, it is set all by itself. There should be no other stones set with it to distract attention unless they enhance the design or appearance of the piece. The jade should be the centrepiece in a piece of jewellery set with other stones. Jade jewellery is best kept clean by rinsing in lukewarm soapy water. Through experience it is found that rinsing jade in brandy, as is done with diamonds, and then rinsing off with lukewarm water is very effective in getting rid of the grease or oil that may have accumulated onto the jade after a period of wear, particularly rings and bracelets or other articles which are in constant touch with the bare skin.

Jade As Ornament & Art

☐ *White jade cicada.*

Understanding Jade

Jade in Art and Art in Jade

The history of Chinese civilization, which is full of folklore and colourful mythology, has given the jade craftsmen an endless array of subjects to display his talents. It can safely be said that there is hardly any object which has not been carved in jade. Similarly there is hardly any art form, design or art symbol that has not been made use of by jade craftsmen in carvings. For a better understanding of the meaning or significance of Chinese symbolic art I have included several pages of designs with brief descriptions of what they are or what they mean. Appreciating beautiful art form is incomplete without knowing its meaning or significance; much like only looking at jade but not enjoying the full tactile sensation of handling jade in one's hands. A word of caution when handling jade though: the stone is fairly brittle and may break under its own weight if dropped on a hard surface.

☐ *Two white jade buckles with dragon designs carved in relief*

Symbolic Art

The following symbolic art forms are included here for reference and understanding. These are the most fundamental of symbolic art commonly met with designs in jade carvings or generally in art, either each by itself or in combination with others
1. Lines and geometric designs
2. Designs derived from ancient traditions
3. Designs derived from Taoism
4. Designs derived from Buddhism
5. Trees and flowers
6. Miscellaneous

The scope of decoration with these symbols is endless.

Lines and geometric designs include

The Pearl Border
Chinese 'T' or key design. This is ancient and can be found on stone urns of the Zhou dynasty second millenium B.C.
Dice pattern
Circles pattern
The Chinese Swastika. Signifies luck, also Chinese for ten thousand.

Designs derived from ancient traditions

The Dragon	The five-clawed dragon was reserved for the Emperor; the four-clawed one for those with royal blood and connection; and the three-clawed variety for the common people.
The Thunder Line	The ancient hieroglyph for thunder shaped like a spiral which later became angular.
The Cloud design	Symbolic and used in conjunction with heavenly bodies or creatures.
Water Design	Symbolic: still water is round; waves are angular.
Fire and Lightning	Shown as scrolls in the shape of blazing flames.
Mountains and Crags	Usually in combination with dragons.
The Ying and Yang	Symbolic of the dual forces of nature.

The Eight Trigrams   Symbol that wards off evil forces.

Designs derived from Taoism

The Eight Immortals
The Phoenix
The Stork
The Peach
The Stag

Designs derived from Buddhism

The Eight Buddhist Emblems of Happy Augury
Flaming Wheel
Conch Shell
Umbrella
Canopy
Lotus Flower
Vase
Pair of Fish
Endless Knot

Other Art Objects

It will suffice for the purpose of this book to relate some of the most common animals that have been carved in jade.

ANIMALS

The twelve animals of the zodiac, namely the Mouse, Ox, Tiger, Hare (or Rabbit), Dragon, Snake, Horse, Goat, Monkey, Cockerel, Dog and Pig.

Mouse

This is a symbol of thrift, and more often the mouse is carved pulling a bunch of grapes, and not just by itself. Sometimes the squirrel is carved in place of the mouse.

Ox

This is a symbol of a hardworking disposition.

Tiger

This is a symbol of power.

Hare

This is a symbol of long life or immortality, and it symbolises the moon.

Dragon

This is a symbol of sovereign power, especially the dragon with 5 claws which was restricted to the Emperor's use in old imperial times.

Snake

This is a symbol of beauty.

Horse

This is a symbol of energy and power.

Goat

This is a symbol of filial piety. The kid kneels to feed on the mother goat's milk.

Monkey

This is a symbol of wisdom.

Cockerel

This is a symbol of punctuality.

Dog

This is a symbol of fidelity and alertness.

Understanding Jade

□ Jade rabbit of the Han dynasty (circa 2nd century A.D.).
Discolouration due to long period of burial in earth.

Jade As Ornament & Art

☐ A magnificent piece of jade carving. The jade cabbage. Note the use of the green portion of the jade as the tip of the leaves.

Understanding Jade

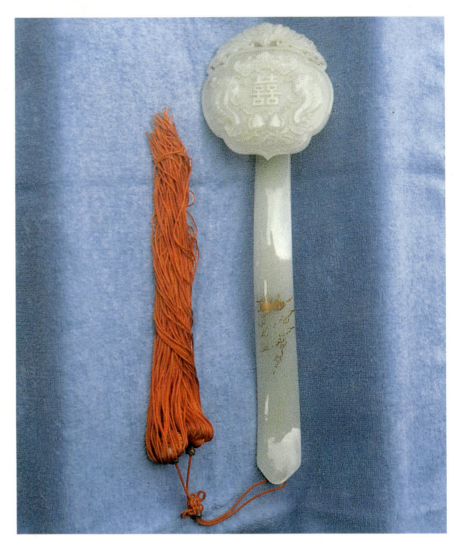

☐ *Pure white Joo-I of excellent quality.*

Jade As Ornament & Art

☐ *The other side of the disc shown at the beginning of the chapter. This is the reverse side which has the carving of the 3-legged toad in the moon sprouting clouds.*

Understanding Jade

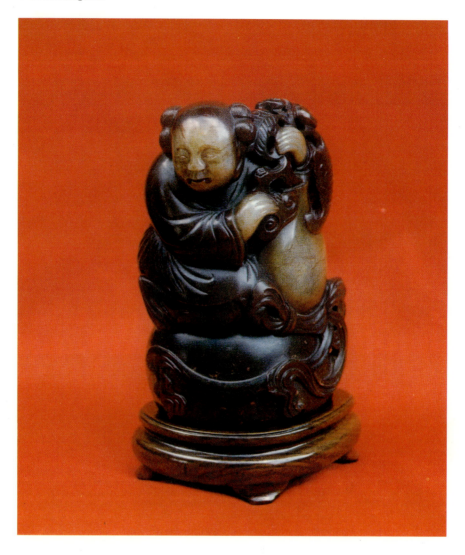

☐ God of Harmony. The craftsmen have ingeniously used the white portion of the jade for the face and hands while leaving the brown for the garment.

☐ A stylised jade bat.

Understanding Jade

□ *An unusual snuff bottle showing an insect carved on its outer profile with a coral stopper.*

Jade As Ornament & Art

□ A white jade pendant of five jade children.

Pig

This is a symbol of satisfaction.

Deer

This animal represents immortality and is often carved with the fungus of immortality *lingzhi* (灵芝) in its mouth.

Bat

This is a symbol of luck or blessing by virtue of its name. It is called *fu* (蝠) which has the same sound as the Chinese word meaning blessing.

Lion

The lion was introduced into China by Buddhism. There were no lions in China. It is a symbol of law and order and protector of sacred buildings like temples and clan buildings.

Fish

This is sometimes represented singly or in pairs when it is intended to be one of the Eight Buddhist Emblems of Happy Augury. The fish is often the carp, a sacred fish, which could come to listen to the preaching of Buddhist scriptures.

Crab

This is merely an object very suitable for presentation in jade because of the beautiful and artistic structure of its body.

Toad

This is a symbol of longevity because of its association with the Moon and the God of Wealth Liu Hai (刘海). The immortal toad in the Moon is a three-legged toad, and the toad held by Liu Hai in his hand is also three-legged.

Insects

Many insects have been carved in jade, especially those with delicate forms which give great scope for the craftsmen to show off their skill. The praying mantis, the butterfly, the bee, the beetle are all favourite subjects.

FRUITS

Like insects, fruits are chosen for their shapes and meaning.

Peach

The peach is a symbol of longevity.

Citron

The citron fruit or Buddha's Hand (佛手), symbolises Buddhism because the fruit resembles Buddha's hand with the index and little finger pointing upwards.

Gourd

Besides its artistic shape, it is a representative symbol of one of the Eight Immortals (八仙), Li Tie Guai (李铁拐).

Grapes

Grapes look beautiful when represented in a bunch, but more artistically with a squirrel pulling or gnawing at them. The colours of jade make it very suitable for grapes.

Pomegranate

This is a symbol of abundance because of its numerous seeds. Here again the colours of jade make it suitable, especially if the outer layer is greenish-yellow and the inside is pink or red.

Understanding Jade

TREES AND FLOWERS

The pine and the willow are favourite subjects. The pine symbolises longevity, often carved together with the stork, and the willow is beauty, mainly womanly beauty.

Flowers are wonderful subjects for the jade craftsmen. The peony is a symbol of wealth. Chrysanthemum is associated with autumn and a life of ease after retirement from public office. The latter association is immortalised by the famous scholar and poet Tao Qian (陶潜), A.D. 365-427, who retired from public office, which he despised, and lived a merry retired life growing chrysanthemums. The lotus is a symbol of purity because it grows out of muddy water and is spotlessly clean. It is the gentleman's symbol.

Bamboo is a symbol of virtue and strong character. The Confucian scholar is often likened to the bamboo which can bend but will not break. Together with the pine and the plum they are called the *Three Friends of Winter* (岁寒三友). These three plants flourish in the winter cold. In carvings they are either carved singly or together, mostly in relief on jade brush holders or on screens, or, in the case of bamboo, with just a short section of the plant with a grasshopper or praying mantis on the reverse.

The Grass of Immortality or *lingzhi* is a very popular object of decoration. It can be carved in a cluster or singly in relief. The most famous representation of this fungus is the *joo-i*, a length of jade carved into a *lingzhi*. Sometimes it is a length of ebony or other hard wood such as rosewood carved into the shape of this fungus with pieces of white jade embedded at three points – the head, the middle portion and the end piece. The most valuable is the single piece of jade *joo-i*, the name *joo-i* meaning 'as you wish'. The origin is vague, but from its name it would appear to be an ornament with an auspicious meaning and handed down as a family heirloom. Some writers say the *joo-i* was originally some sort of weapon made of iron, and later on made of jade and served a very important social purpose such as presents for important persons on special occasions like birthdays or marriages. The carvings will invariably tell the purpose for which the *joo-i* was made. If decorated with carvings of pine, stork or peaches it must be for a birthday because these are symbols of longevity. If decorated with 'double happiness' it must be for a marriage. If decorated with other artistic symbols, then it is probably used for a wider range of happy events, or merely kept as an heirloom. The *joo-i* is a very much sought after possession in families which know its value and significance. A one-foot long white jade *joo-i*, well decorated or plain if the jade is flawless, commands a fabulous price today.

Snuff Bottles

Snuff bottles were originally medicine bottles until snuff was introduced into China from the West in the 16th century. These bottles were quite small originally, but when snuff came to China it became fashionable to take snuff, like smoking tobacco, and snuff bottles became status symbols. The bigger the bottle and the more valuable the material for making it, the higher the status of its owner. It is not generally appreciated that the smaller the snuff bottle the more elegant it is. Most ancient snuff bottles are small ones, the bigger ones were produced much later in the 19th century. They may be of glass, porcelain, ivory, bamboo, or jade and other semi-precious stones. Some of these bottles have very intricate designs and carvings. The most treasured bottles are of jade. There exist in some art centres of the world 'snuff bottle clubs' where members meet regularly to discuss or appreciate and enjoy dainty snuff bottles.

Whereas the collection of antique porcelain has been in vogue and fairly widespread for a comparatively long time, the collection of snuff bottles has been confined to a few connoisseurs and can be said to be somewhat neglected by art collectors until the last century.

Understanding Jade

The Four Spiritually Endowed Creatures (四灵)

These four special creatures are known to almost every Chinese and therefore provide great subjects for art. The *qilin* (麒麟), already described in a previous chapter, the dragon, also already described earlier, the tortoise (龟) and the phoenix (凤). The tortoise is a symbol of longevity, strength and endurance. It has existed since the beginning of 'Chaos' when Pan Gu (盘古) chiselled out the universe. The tortoise is a complete symbolic representation of the universe, its dome-shaped back represents the sky and its belly the earth; they also represent Yang and Ying respectively. Its fabulous longevity together with the markings on its shell gave it a divine status in very ancient times. That is why the tortoise shell is used for divination.

The phoenix is the king of birds, most honoured among the feathered creatures. It appears only in times of peace and great prosperity. It is said to have appeared not more than a few times in Chinese history – first during the reign of the Yellow Emperor (2600 B.C.), then again in Emperor Yao's Palace in 2350 B.C. and again when Confucius was born. It is used as a decorative motif in ceremonial dresses of the empresses of China, just as the dragon is used for the emperors. For this reason some coins were minted during China's history depicting the reign on one side and a pictorial representation of the dragon and the phoenix on the other side. Jade craftsmen have made jade coins of a similar form. Gold craftsmen have also made similar gold coins to add to the delight of art and antique collectors. Jade tortoises are also quite common art objects for connoisseurs of good jade craftsmanship.

Jade's Place in Antiquities

Jade has a recognised and special place in the collection of antiques, according to antiquarians and connoisseurs. There are only four classes of antiques coming within the definition according to Dong Qi Chang (董其昌) A.D. 1555 – 1636 who wrote his famous treatise entitled "Thirteen Narrations on Antiques" (骨董十三说). The first class consists of metal and jade (金玉); the second, calligraphy, painting and carvings (书画墨迹, 石印镌刻); the third, pottery and lacquer ware (窑器漆器); and the fourth, the lute, mirror, sword and inkslabs (琴镜剑砚). Collectors of Chinese antiques who know this subject well follow this classification closely till today.

Jade As Ornament & Art

☐ *A white jade carving of the popular dragon and phoenix motif.*

EPILOGUE

Ancient or old jade has a special place in the classification of antiquities. It is said that collecting and enjoying antiques promotes longevity because the person is in communion with the ancients. This is no myth because collecting and enjoying antiques is a relaxing exercise. In the case of jade there is the added attraction of colour, form and the exquisitely soft touch which is not found in other stones.

One who has a relaxing hobby must invariably live longer than one who is tense most of the time. It has been proven that sickness comes as a result of tension and pressure. Modern life has all the tensions and pressures one can think of. Therefore the collecting of antiques and other more relaxing hobbies and activities are all the more meaningful and beneficial in this modern age.

A person cannot be a collector, in the true and dignified sense of art and antiques, if his object is to make money. If there is a drop or slump in the antique market there will be anxiety and tension among those who collect with the anticipation of making money, just like the effect of the crash in the stock market.

We have seen from ancient times, although recorded writing on jade has been scarce, that jade was an article of utility in prehistoric times – used as axe-heads, arrow-heads and other implements. Then it became an article for use in religious or ceremonial activities, shaped into varying forms. The varied colours were used to fit in with the worship of Heaven, Earth and the Universe according to the seasons, directions and purposes. In those times only the Emperors and other nobles had the sole right to use jade. Then jade came into more general usage as ornaments; and social purposes replaced the religious. Finally came the purpose of personal adornment in the form of jewellery.

Nevertheless the respect and love for jade has not waned or decreased through the centuries. Indeed the respect and love for jade in all forms, both ancient and modern, has never been greater than it is today. Such is the greatness of this Stone Par Excellence in Chinese civilization which has continued for many thousands of years. I am sure posterity will never cease to cherish it.

> "O' Jade
> Thou art the Stone Par Excellence
> For many thousand years.
> For many more thousand years
> to come
> The Excellence is still yours."

BIBLIOGRAPHY

Bishop, H.R.	*Investigations and Studies in Jade.* New York 1906.
Bushell, S.W.	*Chinese Art Vol. 1.* London 1904.
Chen Sheng 陈性	*Yu Ji* (in Chinese). 1911. 玉纪
Chiang Fu-tsung	*Masterworks of Chinese Jade in the National Art Museum.* Taipei 1969.
Ferguson, J.C.	*Survey of Chinese Art,* Chapter V. Shanghai 1939.
Giles, H.A.	*Jades, Adversaria Sinica.* Shanghai 1911.
Laufer, B.	*Jade.* Chicago 1912.
Nott, S.C.	*Chinese Jade Throughout The Ages.* Tokyo, 1962.
Wu Da Zheng 吴大澂	*Gu Yu Tu Kao* (in Chinese). 1889. 古玉图考

DYNASTIES OF CHINA

Period of Five Rulers	五帝	2953 BC - 2205 BC
Xia Dynasty	夏	2205 BC - 1766 BC
Shang Dynasty	商	1766 BC - 1122 BC
Zhou Dynasty	周	1123 BC - 255 BC
Qin Dynasty	秦	255 BC - 206 BC
Han Dynasty	汉	206 BC - AD 221
Three Kingdoms	王国	AD 221 - AD 265
Western Jin Dynasty	西晋	AD 265 - AD 317
Eastern Jin Dynasty	东晋	AD 317 - AD 419
North & South Dynasties (Also Called Six Dynasties)	南北朝 六朝	AD 420 - AD 589
Sui Dynasty	隋	AD 589 - AD 618
Tang Dynasty	唐	AD 618 - AD 907
Five Dynasties	五代	AD 907 - AD 960
Tartar Dynasties	辽	AD 907 - AD 1260
Song Dynasty	宋	AD 960 - AD 1280
Yuan Dynasty (Mongols)	元	AD 1206 - AD 1341
Ming Dynasty	明	AD 1368 - AD 1644
Qing Dynasty (Manchus)	清	AD 1644 - AD 1911
Chinese Republic		AD 1912 -

ABOUT THE AUTHOR

Tan Sri Lee Siow Mong is an expert in Chinese art and culture. He is a renowned exponent of Chinese painting, calligraphy, music and martial arts. A Confucian gentleman in the true sense of the Confucian tradition, his knowledge of things Chinese, vast as it is comprehensive, extends to practical application in daily life. He lectured part-time in the Department of Chinese Studies at the University of Malaya for some ten years, as well as in other bodies and organisations in Singapore and Malaysia. He is a specialist consultant to the Courts in Singapore and Malaysia where he helps settle disputes and doubts in matters concerning Chinese customs and traditions. He has been the President of the China Society of Singapore since 1952.

He led a distinguished career in the civil service in Singapore and Malaysia. He was Permanent Secretary and Director of Education in the Ministry of Education; he was also Permanent Secretary on special duties in the Prime Minister's Department whilst concurrently General Manager of the Public Utilities Board in Singapore. After retiring in 1965, he took up the post of General Manager of the Employees Provident Fund in Malaysia where he remained until 1980 before retiring.

For his dedicated service, he was awarded the Johan Mangku Negara (Commander of the Most Distinguished Order of the Defender of the Realm) in 1974, and the Panglima Setia Mahkota in 1979 (Knight Commander of the Most Distinguished Order of the Crown) by the Malaysian King which carries with it the title of Tan Sri.

An avid collector of jade and other Chinese artifacts, he has written two books, *Spectrum of Chinese Culture*, and *Words Cannot Equal Experience*, his autobiography.

Other books on Chinese subjects published by Times Books International:

Chinese Geomancy, by Evelyn Lip. A layman's guide to the history and theory of geomancy.

Feng Shui for the Home, by Evelyn Lip. The easy guide to understanding and applying Feng Shui for your home or office.

Chinese Temples and Deities, by Evelyn Lip. A fully illustrated study of the constructional styles of some well known temples in China and Southeast Asia.

Chinese Crafts, by Roberta Helmer Stalberg and Ruth Nesi. A highly readable guide to the magnificent ceramic, lacquer, bronze, silk, ivory and jade crafts of China.

Your Chinese Roots, by Thomas Tan Tsu Wee. A book of origins which delves into the patterns of Chinese emigration and the principles which keep these far-flung communities intact.

Straits Chinese Silver, by Ho Wing Meng. A beautifully illustrated collector's guide to this unusual cross-cultural art form.

Straits Chinese Beadwork and Embroidery, by Ho Wing Meng. A highly informative and illustrated description of the origins and use of beadwork and embroidery in the cultural heritage of the Babas and Nonyas.